BITCOIN AND CRYPTO TRADING PRO

Definitions, Risk Management Techniques, Crypto Exchanges, Indicator, and Technical Analysis

WARREN LARSEN

The information contained in this book is for educational and general information purposes only. The content of this volume should not be regarded as advice or recommendation.

The reader will need to consider legal, financial and taxation aspects when evaluating how the information contained in this volume fits their personal circumstances.

Although every precaution has been taken in the preparation of this book, the publisher assumes no responsibility for errors, omissions or damages resulting from the use of the information contained herein.

The author and publisher are not held liable for any loss caused, due to negligence or otherwise, resulting from the use of, or reliance on, the information provided by this book.

Bitcoin and Cryptocurrency Trading Pro: Definitions, Risk Management Techniques, Crypto Exchanges, Indicator, and Technical Analysis

Copyright © 2021 WARREN LARSEN

Written by WARREN LARSEN.

Errors and Feedback

Contact us if you find any errors

Table of Contents

Introduction 1

1. What is Blockchain? 4

2. How Does the Blockchain Work? 8

3. What are Cryptocurrencies? 15

4. History of Bitcoin 21

5. Exchange Cryptocurrencies 29

- LocalBitcoins 31

- The Escrows 34

- Exchange Platforms 37

6. Introduction to Cryptocurrency Trading 43

- How to Read the Graphs 48

- The Technical Analysis 53

- Supports and Resistances 58

- Relative Strength Index (RSI) 63

- Mobile Media 70

- Moving Average Convergence / Divergence (MACD) .. 75

- Ichimoku Cloud 78

- Parabolic Sar..83
7. The Analysis Basic in the Cryptocurrencies Market.............89
8. Conclusion..98

Introduction

In recent years, the world economy, especially thanks to the evolution of technology and information technology, has seen ever greater changes, but above all numerous tools that have joined the already very complex financial world. A very important novelty to be taken into consideration concerns a revolution in general payment systems: the use of *"cryptocurrencies"*. The birth of these digital currencies is to be officially placed in the year 2009, when a boy whose pseudonym is known today, Satoshi Nakamoto, presents for the first time the most famous cryptocurrency but above all the most important for capitalization and not only, **the Bitcoin.** The main reason for the creation of the so-called *"digital gold"* is to be traced back to Nakamoto's desire to create a payment instrument that deviates from a system that had proved to be bankrupt; in fact, the publication of the white paper introducing Bitcoin came just a few weeks after the collapse of the fourth largest investment bank in the United States, Lehman Brothers. From then on, virtual currencies have gradually carved out more and more space among financial instruments, capturing ever greater interest from investors and institutions, both for the functions they perform and for the revolutionary significance in the social sphere. The paper aims to analyze in detail the main characteristics that distinguish Bitcoin and in general, the entire cryptocurrency system, treating a descriptive and analytical study, relating to their treatment in the market.

A guide will come out with the main figures to be analyzed in order to analyze profitable trading scenarios.

The first chapter will evaluate the impacts of the birth and use of blockchain technology, with the events that led to the creation of Bitcoin and therefore, the "Altcoins"

In the following chapters, we will focus on the numerous strengths and weaknesses of digital currencies that for years have divided the critique of economic doctrine, considering the main factors of the very strong financial instability, which for years has caused frequent and intense rises and falls of cryptocurrencies, generating considerable skepticism and distrust on the part of investors.

The central and final part of the work will focus on the research and study of the most common and used indicators for good trading on cryptocurrencies.

Enjoy the reading!

1. What is Blockchain?

The blockchain, quite simply, is nothing more than a distributed database; from Wikipedia, we obtain an easy to understand definition of what a database is, so we are talking about "a data archive structured in order to rationalize the management and updating of information and to allow the carrying out of complex searches". Therefore, by translating this definition into a language that is easily understood by everyone, we are talking about a virtual space in which it is possible to store all kinds of information (economic, but not only).

However, we have said that a blockchain is not simply a database, but a distributed database, what does this mean? Easy, it means that a copy of the information stored in this database is kept on each of the computers that are part of the network. But if a blockchain is nothing more than a database, what makes this technology so revolutionary? Simple, what makes this technology so innovative is the fact that, unlike any other database, the blockchain is substantially armored. To be clear, even the least expert in IT matters knows very well that any IT infrastructure can be hacked, no matter how many security measures you may have, when a database is accessible through the web then it can be hacked; this applies to any archive on the internet,

The reason why this infrastructure cannot be corrupted in any way we will understand better in the course of the next chapters, for now, let's just get familiar with this first concept and that is, a blockchain is basically a distributed and armored database. The fact that this data archive is "distributed" allows us to begin to familiarize with the concept of "decentralization" as well; normally, the databases are "centralized" that is, they are owned by a company or an institution that takes care of updating them, making them accessible to people who may need to consult them and putting in place all necessary security measures, not only to prevent information theft but also to prevent the data stored on that infrastructure from being manipulated and corrupted.

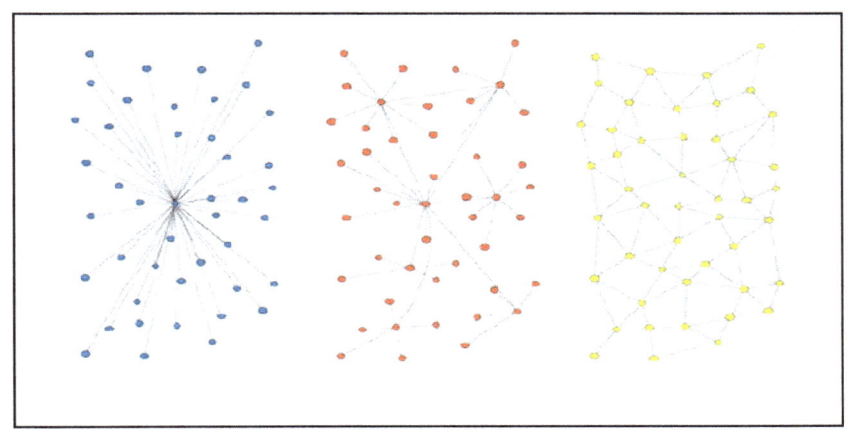

However, since we have said that the blockchain is a distributed database, we understand that there is no "central" body that deals with doing all these things, but all the computers in the network collectively participate in these processes. Simplifying a bit, we can say that there are three types of networks, the "centralized networks" (often also called "star") in which data is transmitted from a central point to all users, the "decentralized networks" in which we begin to have central nodes that transmit information between them without a precise hierarchy and the "distributed networks" in which all the nodes are in communication with each other without a defined hierarchy.

Having understood these first concepts, we already have a way of understanding why blockchain technology is commonly considered the greatest technological innovation after the advent of the internet because for the first time we have at our disposal a perfectly secure database without the need for a central body to manage it and ensure its safety.

2. How Does the Blockchain Work?

In the previous chapter, we explained that a blockchain is a distributed database, now we will try to explain how it works; meanwhile, to make it easier to understand everything, we need to give a concrete example and, therefore, we will talk about the most typical use case concerning this technology, that is the transfer of value (or money) from one user to another. To transfer money from one person to another we are currently all used to using wire transfers; what happens, very simply, is that each bank keeps registers in which it reports the total balance of each account holder and the movements made to and from that particular account.

When I make a transfer (let's say € 100) from my account to that of another person, my bank tracks the movement and marks a transaction of -100 € from my account on its register, then scales this sum from my total balance and send the money to the bank of the person I'm transferring it to.

This, in turn, will do the same by scoring (however, this time on your register) a movement of + € 100 and adding it to the total balance of the account holder who is the beneficiary of the transfer. Exactly the same thing happens with a blockchain, except that the register does not hold it by a bank but (as we have illustrated in the previous chapter) all the computers participating in the network have a copy of this document; for example, when I send a Bitcoin to a person (from here on we will use the abbreviation **BTC** to refer to **Bitcoin** as a currency), all the computers participating in the network mark the movement on the register and deduct 1BTC from my account while, at the same time, add up the same amount for the benefit of the recipient. The first question that arises spontaneously at this point concerns the fact that, since the register is not only shared by all the computers on the network but is also public (that is, it is accessible to everyone in consultation through special sites called "explorer"), anyone could have access to the handling of my account, thus damaging my privacy ; in reality, the accounts (which from now on we will call *"addresses"*) are not attributable to a name and a surname (i.e., to a natural person) but are "strings" consisting of a minimum of 26 to a maximum of 35 alphanumeric characters.

For this reason, bitcoin transactions are said to be anonymous. In reality, this is not even the case, bitcoin is not anonymous but "pseudo-anonymous"; this means, very simply, that although the addresses (that is, we repeat, those we call "current accounts" in the bank) are not registered in the name of real natural persons, it is possible anyway (which does not mean that it is easy that it is possible to do so) follow the computer traces that these transactions leave on the web up to the user (i.e., to the point where the user connected to the internet or the device with which he is connected) and thus define the identity of the natural person who controls that particular address.

Having said that, let's go back to our money transfer and introduce another relevant difference compared to what happens in the banking system; while when I move my money through a bank it immediately traces every transaction and does the same with every other movement, in a blockchain the operations made by the various users are "merged" and inserted into blocks. To understand what a block is, we can imagine it as a box that contains information (sender address, amount handled, recipient address) relating to all transactions "ordered" by users in the unit of time; with Bitcoin, for example, a block is generated every 10 minutes.

Anyone in the course of his life that found himself making an inventory has no difficulty in understanding how this technology works; it is therefore a good metaphor to explain how a blockchain works.

When we do an inventory, all we do is take all the goods we have in stock, put them inside some boxes (numbered in ascending order), and record the contents of each single box on a register. By carefully ordering the different boxes, once the inventory is finished, I will also have a paper "map" that illustrates where each single item is located in the warehouse; if we imagine the inventory of a restaurant that is closing its business, for example, we find all the kitchen utensils (knives, cutlery, plates, pots, glasses, etc.), stored in a warehouse and placed inside boxes. Since the boxes are numbered and I have recorded the contents of each box in the register, whenever I need, for example, the colander, by consulting the register I could know its exact location. A blockchain, therefore, can be thought of as the inventory of all transactions made; in practice, it is nothing more than a huge register that records the trace of all the blocks executed by the network since its inception.

As you read this text, for example, the network is processing a new block and is going to add it to the register of all blocks processed over time. In fact, the term "blockchain" translated into Italian means "chain of blocks" and gives a good idea of how this whole process works; each block registered on the blockchain is linked (like the link of a chain) to the previous one.

This aspect is fundamental to understand why this technology is so reliable, if an attacker tried to manipulate the information contained in one of the blocks already processed by the network, in fact, this modification would cause a series of chain anomalies on all the blocks and the other computers on the network, finding themselves dealing with a document different from the one they have at their disposal, would be able to define the malevolent nature of the operation, thus blocking it instantly. The computers that are part of the network, however, do not limit themselves to transcribing the transactions present within a block on the blockchain, but validate them; when the block is validated by the network it can no longer be modified, the blockchain, therefore, is not only an armored and distributed register (or database) but it is also immutable. At this point, let's stop for a moment to summarize the concepts expressed up to now; when a user wants to transfer money to another user what he does is send the sum from his address to that of the recipient. The information of this single transaction is entered inside a block together with the information relating to all the transactions ordered in the last ten minutes, the network then takes charge of the block, processes it, validates it, and transcribes it on the blockchain.

From that moment on, the information contained in the block becomes immutable and can no longer be modified; easy right? Well, in the next paragraph of this chapter we will illustrate how the network validates and processes the blocks, and above all, we will have the opportunity to understand why the nodes that are part of this network cannot in any way manipulate the information contained in the block that they are processing. In other words, we are going to define who the miners are, what kind of role they have, and why they are so important in the functioning of a blockchain.

3. What are Cryptocurrencies?

After defining what a blockchain is, how it differs from DLT technology, how the validation process of a block works, and what some of the most common consensus protocols that represent the heart of any distributed database consist of, let's move on to deal more strictly on cryptocurrencies; however, we will try to do so not only from a purely technical point of view but also from a philosophical point of view, questioning ourselves on concepts such as that of "value" and "money".

Having said that, let's say right away that giving a definition of what a cryptocurrency is, is not definite; although Bitcoin has existed for ten years, and has given life to a real ecosystem around it, we have not yet been able to find a commonly shared definition of what a cryptocurrency is.

Just take a tour on the web to check how each of the protagonists of this world (the major developers, university professors, CEOs of companies operating in this sector, etc.) who had the opportunity over time to provide their own personal definition of this word without the emergence of one capable of putting everyone in agreement over time.

Consequently, what I will do is provide my definition of what a cryptocurrency is, taking care however (as I am doing right now) to warn the reader that what follows is not THE definition, but A definition of what cryptocurrencies are. Personally, therefore, after a few years of reflection, I came to define a cryptocurrency as "a unit of data whose origin can be established with certainty, who owns it and to which it is possible to attribute a value conventionally accepted by anyone".

To understand what we are talking about, it will be necessary to give concrete examples; we have already mentioned how it is possible to follow every single BTC transaction through websites that take the name of explorer, well, let's go and investigate one of these sites. If we search for "explorer bitcoin" on google, one of the first results is the site "blockchain.com" which shows us, if we just scroll down, a screen listing the succession of the last validated blocks; by clicking on any block, therefore, we can view some information such as the number of transactions it contains, the progressive number that identifies the block (i.e. the height of the block itself), and the total value of the transactions it contains.

What interests us is that each block has a weight, the maximum weight, but it would be better to talk about "maximum size", a BTC block (just to give an example) is 1MB (even if the recent introduction of SegWit has produced a change in this sense, but it is a subject that we will not have the opportunity to adequately deal with in this text); within each block, we find the data relating to each transaction, so we can safely click on one at random to see what information that single transaction contains.

Among the data available to us, in addition to the amount of the exchanged amount, we have the block within which it was validated, the number of confirmations received, the timestamp, the weight, the size, and much more.

Why am I writing all this? Because on the blockchain we go to archive data and that data can be anything, it can be for example a medical record of a patient, it can be the right of ownership in a car, or whatever else we can think of. Currently, if we take the example of Bitcoin, the blockchain records transactions; but what we are calling transactions are basically data, information, and therefore can be any type of information.

A blockchain, in other words, is nothing else than a book that tells a story, more precisely the story it tells is that of the chronological succession of all the transactions processed and validated by the network. If I wanted to create a register of registered cars using a blockchain to which a cryptocurrency was linked, I could easily do it today; in practice, we would have a coin that corresponds to the ownership of a specific car, and on that coin, we would write all the car data (make, model, year of registration, etc.) and the owner's data (year of purchase,

purchase price, name, surname, etc). The day in which the car was sold to a new subject, he would also receive the relative cryptocurrency together with the car on which the data of the new owner would be added.

What we need to do is to stop imagining a cryptocurrency as a dollar bill and start imagining it instead (like a block) as a small box; in that little box you can put anything, any type of information, and at that point, you can also exchange the information with a third party and attribute a value to it on the basis of a convention. When we talk about Bitcoin, for example, each coin is like a small box that contains information, so the question at this point is: what is the information we are trading when we trade a Bitcoin? The information we exchange is the most essential of all, the right of ownership over that box (basically the coin) that we exchanged; when I send a Bitcoin from my address to another person's address, the information that is stored on the blockchain in that coin (not another, not any of those in circulation, but exactly that coin) ceases to be owned by my address (i.e. mine) and becomes the property of a new address (i.e. the person controlling that new address). How can we be sure of the unique ownership of the coin? Because we have its private key.

4. History of Bitcoin

In the previous chapter, we had the opportunity to mention how, over the years, Bitcoin has begun to build a sort of "standard" comparable to that of gold so that every time the economy of a state begins to show signs of weakness we can witness an increase in cryptocurrency trading volumes in that particular country; this, in hindsight, it is a trait that has characterized Bitcoin since its inception.

It was in 2008 when a character who signed himself under a pseudonym made his appearance proposing a global currency supported by a P2P network in conjunction, and in a certain sense in response, to the banking scandals that earned the honor of the news by following one another and substantially representing the beginning of the great economic crisis that will then infect the economies of the rest of the world; this character, whose true identity is still unknown ten years later, will go down in history under the pseudonym of Satoshi Nakamoto.

More precisely, Satoshi makes his appearance in November (2008) by publishing on "The Cryptography mailing list" (on the site "Metzdowd.com") a document concerning the consent protocol that will allow Bitcoin to function; a few months later (in 2009), the first version of the software was distributed and other developers started working on it. A little more than a year after the birth of Bitcoin (in 2010), Satoshi withdraws from the community, his last public message dates back to 2011 and serves to communicate the handover to Gavin Andresen.

This is perhaps the strangest thing about this technology, that the person who basically invented it (even if not out of nowhere) was able not only to remain anonymous all this time, but even decided to completely exit the scene within less than two years after giving life to his creation; that Satoshi Nakamoto ends up in school books as a notable personality, he has already ended up there to tell the truth, there is no course in any University in the world where we talk about blockchain and cryptography without mentioning Satoshi.

The important thing to understand when we think of Satoshi is that we are talking about one of the brightest minds of this century, the mathematics that supports Bitcoin and allows it to work, in fact, is commonly considered so advanced that many have come to argue that behind the pseudonym of Satoshi Nakamoto, there is not a single person but a team of hackers with very solid skills; not even of this (i.e., of the "collective" nature behind the figure of Satoshi) we have proof or confirmation, so the figure of this person is still shrouded in mystery.

In a good Netflix documentary (Banking on Bitcoin, 2016), we can find one of the most plausible reconstructions of how things went; to create Bitcoin, therefore, it should have been one of the major exponents of the cypherpunk movement, so inevitably one or more between Nick Szabo, Hal Finney, Adam Back and Wei Dai. The cypherpunk, which probably almost no one has ever heard of in our country, if not perhaps a few "enthusiasts", was a countercultural movement made up informally of people interested in privacy which aimed to achieve individual freedom through the use of cryptography; The ideological approach that these groups have always had has been of a libertarian character, oscillating between social anarchism, anarcho-individualism, and anarcho-capitalism.

Even today, in 2018, the anarchist component in the world of cryptocurrencies is clearly recognizable, despite the fact that in this world there are large banks, national institutions, entrepreneurs, and ordinary people who in any way can be defined except anarchists. In any case, this technology has its roots in a cultural humus (the anarchist one) which still represents the common thread through more than a decade of technological development. But let's go back to Satoshi's identity, "Banking on Bitcoin" reconstructs who that may be to me (and many others), seems to be very likely; behind the pseudonym of Satoshi Nakamoto there would be Hal Finney (a leading exponent of cypherpunk in the USA), who fell ill with ALS in 2011 and died in 2014 at the age of 58.

There was also a time when an Australian entrepreneur (Craig Steven Wright) seemed to be the real Satoshi but soon this too was discarded. Some might say at this point that obviously Satoshi has now disappeared, having become rich, will have converted all his Bitcoins into dollars and will be spending the rest of his days sipping Cuba libre in the Maldives; in reality what are the addresses owned by Satoshi we know very well, and on these addresses, hundreds of Bitcoins are blocked that have not been moved for years. This is what leads us to suspect that Satoshi may be Hal Finney himself (who died in 2014) because there was a moment when Bitcoin prices went up to $20,000, in which even only 100BTC has reached a value of 2 million dollars (and more than 100BTC are blocked on Satoshi's addresses overall); the fact that all this money has been stuck on their respective addresses all these years without ever being moved suggests the idea that simply the owner of those Bitcoins (i.e., Satoshi) has passed away.

Given that we will never know the true identity of Satoshi Nakamoto, who we almost always take for granted that he is a man but he could be a woman, he could even be a Martian for all we know, Bitcoin already appears (in just ten years from his birth) having been able to outlive its inventor; and all this despite having lived very bloody moments in the course of his young life. As I write this text, for example, Bitcoin has lost about 80% of its value compared to the last peaks of January 2018 and this leads many detractors to argue that its end has come; what the detractors do not say is that Bitcoin has already had a bad time several times in the course of its history, showing each time that it has broad enough shoulders to come out stronger than before. The first major collapse in Bitcoin history was already in 2011 when, after a mad rush that in a few months swelled the price from $0.92 to the exorbitant figure of $ 32 per coin, Bitcoin prices collapsed again around $2. "Now, it's over." the experts said, "Bitcoin is dead" the newspapers ruled; but things did not go like this, the following year (2012), Bitcoin immediately offered the first signs of strength, returning to quote around $7. Already in mid-January, however, a new slap pushed him down by almost 40%; however, it seemed to be a trivial correction, since the summer of the same year the prices returned to close to $15, except that a new bearish wave pushed the price down another 50%.

In short, when it seemed that Bitcoin would never recover its historical peak of 2011, the price exploded again, marking, in the spring of 2013, a new high close to $50. In the following months, BTC will resume its run with new highs close to $100 this time first and then, with the new all-time high recorded in April 2013, touching $270.

Bitcoin is unstoppable, it cannot be stopped, it will be worth thousands of dollars, the most enthusiastic said, and instead Bitcoin returned down, only a few days after hitting the new high, reaching $67 in the same month of April. At this point, prices enter a lateral phase, prices remain fairly stable around $120 until the end of the year when a new bull run starts that drags the price up to $1100. Wow! Too bad that within a few weeks the price will return to plummet, this time settling at $500 and remaining in a kind of sideways for the next 18 months. Thus we arrive at 2014, another annus horribilis for our cryptocurrency which, in the meantime, has climbed to almost touching the $900 level; the perfect storm, though.

The reaction of the markets to all this is understandably a kind of massacre, the price of Bitcoin plunges again and stands at $400, where it remains stationary for another couple of years. We, therefore, come to more recent times, when finally in January 2017 Bitcoin returns to break the $1000 wall and begins a race that will lead it, between December 2017 and January 2018, to touch a new all-time high of around $20,000. Since that moment, Bitcoin has entered a new bearish phase, reaching lows of around $3,000 and giving a new voice to the detractors who once again rushed to affirm that "this time, it is the very end"; who among the detractors and supporters will have the last word is still early to say until today.

Whether this will happen again or if it happened for the last time in 2017 is too early to say, time will surely give us an answer, so just arm yourself with patience and watch what happens.

5. Exchange Cryptocurrencies

With the birth of Bitcoin, the need arose to exchange the new cryptocurrency with fiat currency; from the beginning, those who wanted to understand what this new currency consisted of had only two ways to do it, or get hold of some Bitcoin by mining it (which was initially much easier than it is today) or do it by buying it from someone who already owned it.

Then, over time, some traders began to accept this new form of payment, they too needed to convert that profit made in BTC into legal tender currency; even the most avid supporters, those who have kept their BTC for the longest, have also had the opportunity to spend them over time.

Today, spending our cryptocurrencies has become extremely easy, thanks to cards which allow us to instantly convert our cryptocurrencies by withdrawing cash at any ATM, but we have arrived at all this over time, through an evolution that has lasted years. As anyone can imagine, initially there was not even a real market as there is today, at the beginning, there was only Bitcoin and the simplest way to convert it into fiat currency was to physically exchange it for cash; obviously bartering was not a very rational way to manage it, so soon the first exchange platforms were born, what everyone commonly calls exchanges and which today allow us to easily exchange even large volumes of cryptocurrencies.

In the next chapter, we will talk about just this, about how it is possible to exchange cryptocurrencies between individuals, about the platforms on the internet that allow you to do this type of operation, and about some particular sites that allow us to exchange even large amounts of cryptocurrencies with currencies, guaranteeing total security despite the fact that we find ourselves working with complete strangers; all this, ultimately, is part of what until now we have called the "cryptocurrency ecosystem", a layered and complex reality of services that allow users to manage their cryptocurrency, to exchange it and to use it to buy goods and services.

- **LocalBitcoins**

If from the first moment it seemed obvious that the simplest way to exchange cryptocurrencies was in person, basically going to buy Bitcoin using cash, would build a "market" of this type (therefore based on a sort of barter), therefore, resorting to the web was an equally obvious choice. The very success of the internet, not surprisingly, had also passed through all those services (still today there are dozens of them) that allow the sale between private individuals, in which there is someone who places an ad and someone else who got the ad responds.

With Bitcoin, things went exactly like this, even today there is a site called Localbitcoins (online continuously since 2012) that connects those who buy and sell cryptocurrencies locally. through Localbitcoins (and other similar sites), however, supply and demand are limited to meeting, that is, they have a first approach, while the real currency exchange is managed in person, typically in cash. In big cities, it is not difficult to find someone who also wants to buy significant amounts (up to a few thousand euros) of cryptocurrencies by paying them with cash, but it is no less difficult to suffer scam attempts in this way; in fact, there are not a few people who, for having exchanged their cryptocurrencies in this way, have found themselves in their hands a few thousand euros of fake money.

When proceeding with this type of exchange, it is always preferable to have the necessary precautions and never take anything for granted; the risk of being faced with people willing to scam us exists and must always be taken into consideration. Although it may seem unsafe, this type of exchange is still very much in vogue today, above all because the job offer also moves through these channels; in fact, there are many people around the world who have cryptocurrency to spend and would like to invest it in their project.

Obviously, it is not common to find advertisements on these platforms to be a baker, but there are numerous ones related to translation jobs, the creation of websites and smartphone applications, as well as a very large number of job advertisements related to the blockchain (issue a token, create a smart contract, write articles for specialized sites, etc). All this testifies to the revolutionary door of this technology, around the blockchain was born much more than a simple market, a real economy was born with lots of jobs, university courses with secure professional outlets, projects financed for millions of euros; unthinkable today that such a technology, with all its potentials, is not yet clearly expressed.

The existence of sites such as Localbitcoins shows us how the "crypto-economy" (I think we can easily get used to calling it that from now on), contrary to what its detractors claim, is not based on nothing but rests instead on concrete foundations and it is supported at different levels; it is frankly impossible to think that people who have already come into contact with this technology, who have understood how it works and who already use it regularly can stop doing it in the next ten years, while it is not difficult to imagine that in a similar period of time more and more people may decide to start using it for the most varied reasons with any of the hundreds of cryptocurrencies currently available on the market.

- **The Escrows**

If in any big city in the world finding someone who wants to exchange cryptocurrencies is all in all quite simple, in small towns, this is not as easy; despite this I myself, who also live in a small town in southern Italy, in 2016 I was surprised by the fact that there was a person less than 2km from me who wanted to sell 3BTC.

To be honest, that person was also the only one in the whole province, so it was clearly a coincidence that he was right near my house and maybe, why not, it could also be an attempted scam (this I will never have a way of knowing for sure not having responded to that announcement). To all this we must add that in many countries banks are, understandably, reluctant to favor the movement of money towards cryptocurrencies and tend to block incoming and outgoing transfers connected to the accounts of some large exchange platforms; so how can you exchange cryptocurrencies even for significant amounts through the internet and without risking taking the proverbial package? Simple, we use special services called "escrow". On the internet, in fact, there are dozens of sites that allow you to do exactly this; the system is as simple as it is ingenious.

These sites are nothing more than a catalog of third parties who take on the responsibility of managing the transaction on behalf of all the parties involved; each of these users has a rating and, of course, requires a fee to carry out such a delicate task. The commission required by each escrow varies according to the rating that the user has accumulated, a bit like on e-bay, therefore, the rating defines the quality of the service offered; it is therefore quite reasonable to pay a higher commission to those users who have concluded the highest number of transactions over time, for amounts of all kinds, always leaving the parties fully satisfied.

It goes without saying that an inexperienced user could, following a mistake, have attributed the loss of their cryptocurrencies to escrow, thus attributing a negative rating to it. The reasons why an escrow can receive a negative rating are many, not just bad fate, so it is not so obvious for a user to receive a good rating. Having ascertained this, what kind of activity does the escrow perform? Simply the users who perform this function act as a bridge between the two parties, those who want to sell their Bitcoins, for example, send them to the escrow address which, to complete the sales process, waits to get hold of the relative amount in euros (to give an example) of those who want to buy those BTCs instead. When the escrow is in possession of both sums of money, after having obviously withheld his commissions, it proceeds to forward the amount due to the relative owners and concludes the exchange; in a system of this type, the escrow has no incentive to cheat the parties by disappearing with the swag, because this would forever undermine their credibility, preventing them from continuing to profit from this activity.

With this system, therefore, scams become extremely rare and difficult, excluding the risk that escrow can act in bad fate since they are paid for not doing so, even if one of the parties were willing to try a scam, it could never succeed to complete it without the participation of the escrow itself.

This system, of course, is not exactly the cheapest of all and probably not even the most comfortable way to exchange fiat currency for cryptocurrencies, however, it has been used by thousands of users who have testified to its quality and effectiveness for years now.

- **Exchange Platforms**

There are many reasons why you may want to trade cryptocurrencies (with other cryptocurrencies or with fiat currency) and there are also many different ways to do it; what you need to be clear in mind is that there is a right way to satisfy every different need. Not understanding, this simple thing when dealing with cryptocurrencies can lead to unpleasant inconveniences;

a very common mistake, for example, is that the function of an exchange platform (or exchange if you prefer) is to allow the conversion of different cryptocurrencies into other currencies or fiat currency.

In reality, this type of service was created to allow trading and not to simply allow you to change your currencies. For example, imagine a lawyer who agrees to be paid also in cryptocurrency; since only a few clients decide to pay him this way, the lawyer tends not to spend that money and eventually accumulates a tidy sum on his Bitcoin address.

At some point, inevitably, our lawyer will want to spend this sum, and perhaps instead of spending his coins as they are, he decides, even a little lazily, that the time has come to convert them into euros; what is the most comfortable way to do it? Well, just open an account on one of the largest and most reliable trading platforms on the market and transfer the BTCs to their address, at which point you place a sell order in euros and that's it; quite right? Mistaken! Or rather, things won't necessarily turn out to be that simple. When our handsome lawyer tries to transfer the sum just converted into euros to his current account, the account could be frozen. Why? Why didn't he read the compliance rules!

Obviously, not all exchanges adhere to this type of protocol, without this implying that their activity is in some way considered illegal, it simply depends on the different rules that different countries apply to manage this type of market. In Italy, for example, opening an exchange requires adapting to very stringent rules and is therefore not a simple (and even less economical) activity to start.

This set of rules, which takes the name of compliance, provides among other things, in addition to the identification of users (which is why today almost all platforms require the sending of user documents) also that the funds deposited are used specifically for trading; did our lawyer think he could just exchange his BTC? Our lawyer was wrong! Since his behavior is considered improper and expressly prohibited by the regulation of the platform (yes, just what no one reads when opening an account on any website), our handsome lawyer found his account frozen.

This does not mean that it is not possible to use an exchange platform to change our Bitcoin, that of the lawyer is just one example of the risks that a lazy person takes when he does not do things with due attention, but there are numerous exchanges on the market, even among the largest, which do not have such strict rules; so our lawyer was also a bit unfortunate, not that it matters, he got into a big deal and will take months to get out of it (assuming he can).

The world of cryptocurrencies, this should be quite clear by now, is however definitely refractory to the regulations imposed from above, hence the fact that users (including traders themselves) are forced to sacrifice their privacy in order to operate legitimately with their coins (since they have to submit their documents to exchange platforms to open an account), it's not exactly one of the most popular norms within the community; at a certain point, users, on social networks and on forums, through blogs, began to tell each other that it would not be a bad idea to build a decentralized exchange.

After all, what else is an exchange platform if not an updated register of all the exchanges made? Exactly the type of data that can be processed through a blockchain, as long as there is a decentralized network of nodes that guarantees its functioning. At this point anyone can guess why at this very moment on the market there are at least a dozen platforms (with related native cryptocurrencies in tow) that offer exactly this service; users can then transfer their coins to these platforms and do their own trading (or just simply change their coins) exactly as they currently do with large centralized exchanges. Where is the difference? In this way, they can do it anonymously and in many cases, without paying commissions for every operation they make; a nice advantage, no doubt about it.

To make this even easier to do, a recent innovation has also contributed, which takes the name of "atomic swap", and which allows, in simple terms, to use a smart contract to process an exchange of currencies between coins belonging to different chains; in this exchange, the smart contract essentially acts as a real escrow (thus protecting both parties involved) making sure to send the coins to the relevant valid addresses. Let's imagine that a user wants to buy ETH using their BTC; a smart contract will take its BTC, it will search for one or more users capable of satisfying the request at the price set by the user and as soon as this is possible it will self-execute by paying the respective parts to the addresses that each of them will have previously established.

That of decentralized exchanges is one of the best examples to demonstrate the advantages of disintermediation which, inevitably, also coincides with a drop in the costs incurred by the end-user; the reduction of costs, then, becomes an extraordinary incentive to convince more and more users to abandon centralized models in favor of decentralized ones and that is why, at least in the long term, all this new technology based on disintermediation and decentralization seems inexorably destined to win over the (centralized) models that currently regulate some of the main aspects of our social life.

6. Introduction to Cryptocurrency Trading

Inserting an in-depth chapter dedicated to trading in a text that deals with blockchain and cryptocurrencies is in my opinion, something inevitable; one of the advantages of this technology is that all those who discover it immediately feel the need to begin to understand how the market works.

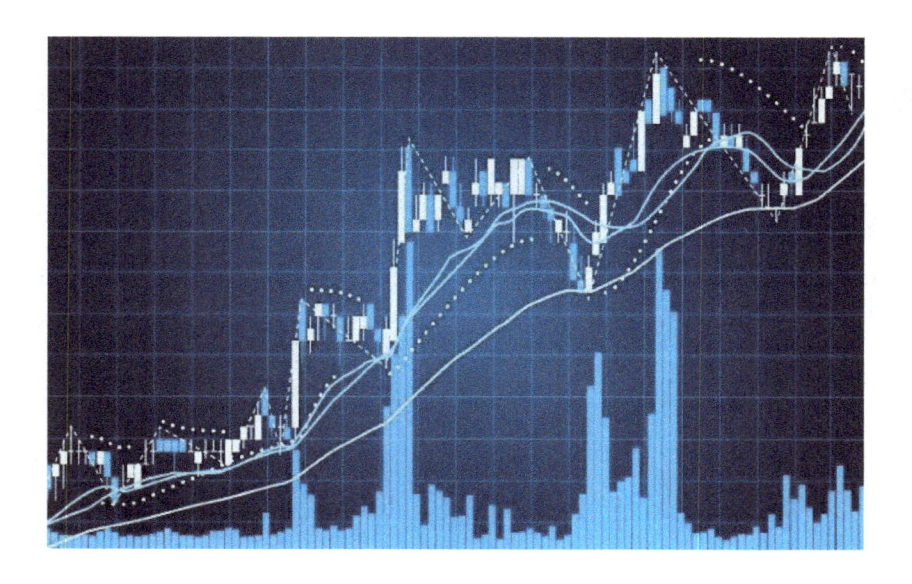

The reasons that push a person to start trading cryptocurrencies can be different, there are those who do it out of pure curiosity, those to better understand the same technology, those simply because they see the possibility of earning money, in any case, it is extremely common for those who approach cryptocurrencies almost simultaneously decide to open a trading account on an exchange platform.

This has allowed many people to acquire the basic rudiments of economic-financial education, a form of education which is almost completely absent in our country and which would be badly needed; the "quantum" leap that people who start using Bitcoin and other cryptocurrencies make is that, since they have full control of their money, they can also freely invest it. And for the rest, as I like to say whenever I have the chance, "even a monkey can make a profit by trading"; what does this activity consist of? I think one word is enough to say it and that word is "rules"; trading is a system of rules. I try to be clearer; the value of a given currency changes continuously when referred to the value of a second currency.

What a trader does is to take advantage of these value swings to make a profit, buy BTC at a low price (for example at $100) and resell at a higher price (for example at $120); the difference between the selling price and the buying price represents the profit (or loss) realized with that single operation. If I buy 1BTC at $100 and sell it for $120, I have earned $20, if on the contrary I buy 1BTC at $ 120 and sell it at $100, I will have lost $20.

In cryptocurrency trading, we can observe two major trends, that of traders who always operate in pairs with a fiat currency (for example, they buy BTC to earn Dollars) and those who trade in cryptocurrencies (they buy any altcoin to earn BTC); the person who operates in the first way (that is, accumulates dollars) is a person who is probably convinced that the supremacy of fiat currencies will never be affected by cryptocurrencies, consequently uses price changes to earn more legal tender currency. The person who instead operates in the second way (i.e., accumulates Bitcoin) is a person who is convinced that, regardless of what happens during bearish cycles, Bitcoin is destined in the long term to continue to increase its value, always hitting new peaks. Regardless of the way in which it operates, there are some essential things you need to know.

1. Scalping: means that the trader opens and closes numerous transactions during the same day,

aiming to make a profit in the shortest possible time by exploiting even the smallest price changes

2. Day trading: in this case the trader tends to make much less operation, rarely exceeding two or three in the same day and as a basic rule each operation is opened and closed strictly within 24 hours

3. Swing trading: those who do this type of trading reduce the number of operations even more than the day trader and as a basic rule the duration of the trade is extended from one day (maximum duration of day trading) up to ten days (indicatively the maximum time frame within which the single transaction should be closed)

4. Cassettista: operates more according to an investment logic than (as in other cases) in a purely speculative logic; between when the drawer opens an operation and when he closes it, months can easily pass; moreover, it is difficult for this type of operator to manage more than two or three investments at the same time.

In general, a good trader knows how to adapt his operations to all these four trading styles based on the market trend; therefore, depending on the moment the trader decides to adopt one style instead of another, the same trader who is scalping today could then suddenly adopt a swing trading logic and then go back to scalping once the previous operations are closed.

As we said, trading is basically a system of rules, once these rules are set correctly, you inevitably start to make a profit; this does not mean that you will easily become a billionaire, but simply that you will be able to make your savings relatively easily. The difficult thing when we talk about trading is not even learning the technique (which after all is accessible to anyone), but having full control of one's psychology.

Each trader is in fact constantly exposed to a great psychological pressure that induces him, regardless of the rules he has given himself, to sell or buy in an unreasonable way; the point is that no matter how good you are, all traders are trading at a loss, a good trader simply accumulates more profit than loss. The psychological reactions of each operator can be different and can change, as well as from person to person, from situation to situation; therefore, there are no rules valid for everyone to manage the most demanding aspect (which is the psychological dimension) of the trading activity.

In the next paragraphs, therefore, in addition to describing the functioning of some fundamental tools in the activity of each trader, we will also try to make more general reflections on this type of profession to offer each reader a broad point of view and a sufficient basis. solid from which to start if you want to try your hand at this type of activity.

- **How to Read the Graphs**

Finding yourself trading when you discover cryptocurrencies is a very common thing, the fact that those who approach this type of activity do so thinking of becoming immensely rich in record time is unfortunately the same. Even if anyone can learn to exploit the market cycles to make a profit, it is not certain that all those who engage in this activity will reach the goal; as mentioned in the previous paragraph, in fact, trading is a system of rules but since we impose these rules on ourselves, most of the time we end up deciding to infringe them. In any case, the first rule that every trader must follow is "never invest more than you are willing to lose"; this is the only way to prevent the psychological pressure we will be subjected to become unmanageable.

The first thing we must do, therefore, is to learn to read stock market charts which, in jargon, are called "Japanese candlestick charts"; obviously the price trend can also be graphically rendered by a straight line, however, the candlestick charts give us much more information than we could obtain by observing a line.

The reason why these graphs are called this way is quite intuitive, the graphical signs (those colored red and green) in fact resemble candles; the first thing we must understand to correctly interpret this type of chart is that each candle expresses the price trend in the unit of time defined by the user. Precisely for this reason we hear about charts for one hour, four hours, one day, one week and so on, because it means that each of the candles that appear on the chart represents what happened to the price over a period of time of one hour, four hours, one day and so on.

Now, let's imagine reading a 1D (one day) chart, we know that each candle graphically represents what happened over the last 24h; very simply, therefore, if the candle is colored red this means that in the twenty-four hours the price has dropped, on the contrary, if the candle is colored green it means that the price has gone up.

Two other data that the candle represents graphically are the opening and closing prices which are represented by the lower and upper edges of the candle; when we read a red candle (which signals a drop in price in the unit of time) the upper border indicates the opening price and the lower one the closing price of the session. When we read a green candle (which signals the price increase in the unit of time) is the exact opposite, in this case, the lower edge of the candle indicates the opening price and the upper one the closing price.

In some cases, we can observe candles that are not colored and substantially resemble crosses, this type of candle indicates that the opening price was substantially identical to the closing price; the edges of these crosses (directed upwards or downwards) graphically represent the price changes (maximum and minimum) that occurred during the session. To summarize, a candle can be colored red (when the closing price is lower than the opening price) or green (when the closing price is higher than the opening price), the perimeter of these candles (called "body") represents the opening and closing levels in the unit of time, while the straight lines starting from the top or bottom of the candle represent the peaks, respectively maximum and minimum that was touched during a session.

Let's take some practical examples and imagine that the price of 1BTC after starting from a price of $10 at the opening touched a maximum of $15 and then closed the session at $12, how is all this represented by the candle? Simple, in the meantime, we will have a green candle (because the price has risen), similar to a rectangle whose lower edge is positioned at $10 (the opening) and the upper edge is positioned at $12 (the close); from the upper margin, then, we will see starting a straight line (called in jargon "shadow") that reaches $15.

Another example, but this time let's imagine that the opening price is $20 and the closing price is $17 with the day's low at $15 and the day's high at $22; in this case, the candle will be red (session at a loss), the upper margin (opening price) will be positioned at $20, from here the upper shadow (the straight line) will start, representing the high of the day and which will touch share $22, while the lower margin of the candle (closing price) will settle at $17, the level from which the lower shadow (always another straight line) will start and will reach the low of the day at $15.

The last example, finally, a session that opens and closes at $17, corresponding to the low of the day and with a maximum peak reached of $20; in this case, the candle will look like a cross, therefore it will not have any color because the opening and closing price coincides, there will be no lower shadow because the low of the day has never gone below the opening but there will be a long upper shadow that it will extend up to $20.

Everything that we have illustrated in words up to now can be found summarized in the image below which will allow you to better understand all the new terminology we have introduced.

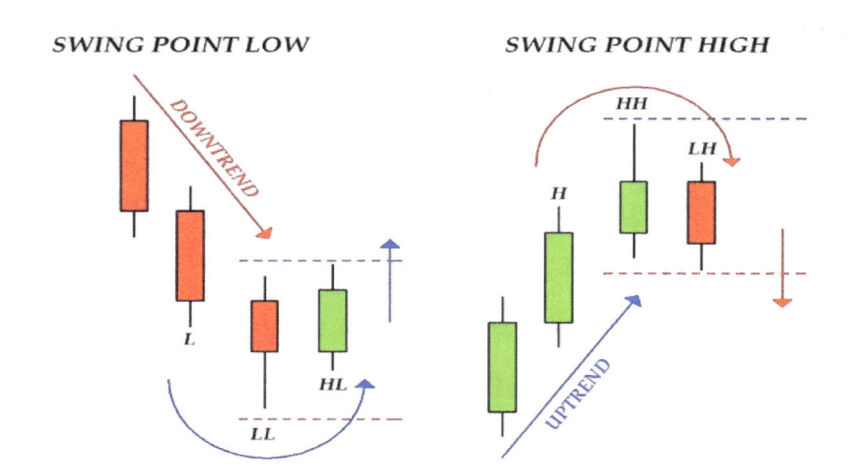

- **The Technical Analysis**

Even if you wouldn't say it, in these few paragraphs we have already acquired several fundamental concepts for trading, in the meantime, we have learned how to read a candlestick chart, then we began to understand that trading means creating your own system of rules; this aspect is fundamental because without an effective system of rules we will never be able to make a profit and we will fail on all our trades.

The purpose of these rules, however, is not to allow you to make a profit but rather to allow the trader to ease the psychological pressure to which he will inevitably be exposed until the moment in which he closes the operation; on the other hand, to establish how to make a profit, each operator is based on what is essentially a real "collection of signals".

The first question that every person inevitably asks themselves when they start trading is: what moves the price of a cryptocurrency? Finding a good answer to this question already means you have taken the first step in becoming a good trader. The price is mainly driven by two factors namely, the greed of the market and the news breaking into the market; these two factors, taken together, generate the price movements that allow us to make a profit.

When we begin to operate on a particular market, regardless of the type of market, any news concerning it can trigger a bullish or bearish reaction in the price trend; this always applies and obviously also applies to cryptocurrencies.

There are news, such as the possibility of a hard fork or the release of a new version of the platform (with new features), which inevitably trigger the rise in prices, other news, however, do the exact opposite and sink the value of a coin; if the news spreads that the official wallet of a certain currency is defective or that a certain cryptocurrency is about to be excluded ("delisted" in jargon) from a large platform, these are news capable of causing large losses at the price of a crypto.

If understanding how and why news moves the market is easy enough, it is more difficult to understand the way in which the greed of operators causes price fluctuations; first of all, what we must understand is that the price trend is never linear, better than as a straight line, in fact, we would do well to imagine it as a wave that oscillates between minimums and maximums.

When we begin to imagine the price trend as if it were a wave, we begin to frame two different trends, one short-term in which the price moves between minimums and maximums within what is called a "channel" (we will see later what it is), and at the same time, we find a second trend in progress, more long-term, which sees the price destined to increase or decrease.

There are obviously several tools available to traders to recognize these trends in the price trend (some of which we will get to know later) but in principle, the dynamics we are witnessing are always the same; since all traders pursue the same goal (to make a profit) and all read the same chart at the same time, when certain conditions occur, all traders will click en masse to take advantage of the opportunity and here, as mentioned, the greed of the market ends up moving the price.

However, this is also true on the contrary, the fears of the market, therefore, can cause, in the presence of certain circumstances, a wave of sales that can lead the individual trader to suffer even significant losses. The ability to read the market trends through the price trend on a chart, to recognize the moments of reversal (both short and long term) in the main trend (regardless of whether it is bullish or bearish), all this passes under the name of "technical analysis"; what the trader does, in other words, is to use the tools at his disposal to define the pattern of the trend and try to make a profit on the basis of price changes.

The bad thing about technical analysis is that it is not an exact science but more of a statistical calculation; none of the data we get from reading the charts ever gives us guarantees, although there are more relevant (and more reliable) signals than others, there are no 100% safe trading signals; moreover, every good trader naturally oscillates between a speculative approach and a more moderate one based on investment, consequently, a complete operation on the market technical analysis is not sufficient but it is necessary to support it with fundamental analysis.

All the concepts we are exposing exist on every type of market, the charts read the same way both on the forex and on the cryptocurrency market, the technical analysis is the same whether you are investing in stocks or buying coins and also with regard to fundamental analysis, it is a concept that always exists, regardless of the type of market we are operating in.

When we buy shares, for example, the fundamental analysis consists in reading the balance sheet of the company in which we are going to invest; in the cryptocurrency market, this time unlike what happens in other markets, fundamental analysis is done by collecting information of a different nature, as we will see better in one of the next paragraphs. For now, let's focus on knowing some elementary tools that every trader normally uses in his daily practice to search for trading signals that allow him to make a profit.

- **Supports and Resistances**

We have said that the price moves like a wave within a long-term trend that can be bullish (Englishism used to indicate bullish trends) or bearish (a term that indicates bearish trends); quite simply in a bull market, the price tends to always touch new peaks, while in a bear market it tends to always touch new lows.

When in the midst of a well-defined trend the price fails to touch a new peak (minimum or maximum), that is the first sign of a weakening of the trend and indicates that we could be close to a reversal of the main trend.

If we then graphically combine the maximum peaks reached by the price with a straight line and do the same for the minimum peaks, we graphically obtain important levels at the level of technical analysis; these levels are called support (when we speak of the line that joins the minimum peaks) and resistance (when we speak of the line that joins the maximum peaks).

In a very intuitive way, when the price is near a support this represents a difficult level to break down and therefore it is easy that (in the short-term trend) the price is going to rebound; in the same way, when the price is near the resistance, representing that a level is difficult to break upwards, it is easy for the price to begin to slide down going to look for the first useful support again. However, we must always consider that the more times these levels are tested (i.e., they are reached by the price), the less likely it becomes that they can withstand the next wave; when the price starts beating against a resistance sooner or later it is likely to be able to break it and therefore start to rise, and the same obviously applies to supports.

In this dynamic that we have just described, there are two relevant moments for a trader's activity, when the price is near those price levels that we have called supports and resistances and when the price breaks these levels. Given that today there are financial instruments that allow you to make a profit even when the price is falling (short sale), it would be preferable for a novice trader to concentrate on making all upward operations and then later, only after having had a fair amount of experience, also integrate more advanced tools into their operations.

Our neophyte crypto trader who wants to make a profit with the upward variations of the price has two ideal moments to open a position and precisely when the price is near a support and when the price breaks a resistance; opening a position by counting on the rebound near the support is a strategy that often allows you to make a profit but which presents greater risks since it is not said that the support will hold, instead, opening the position when it has broken upwards the resistance is a more moderate trading strategy, which allows us to take less risk and therefore inevitably offers us less profit opportunities.

The truth is that in any case, despite how sophisticated our market analysis skills are, no one can really predict where the price is going; this is always true, even more so in a market like that of cryptocurrencies which is subject to continuous manipulation. In fact, since the cryptocurrency market (especially for some coins) is not very liquid, some operators with large financial capacities are in the position of being able to provoke speculative maneuvers that are defined in jargon as "pump and dump", that is, they accumulate large quantities of coins at a certain price for weeks and then, suddenly injecting enormous volumes of liquidity, favor a rise in prices that it will allow them to subsequently resell to other operators what was previously accumulated at a lower price.

Having completed the speculative maneuver and painfully trimmed the package to all the operators who had rushed to chase that sudden rise in the price of the currency, and lacking the liquidity that had allowed the rise, the price falls back down (together with the mood of the operators who fell victim to the speculative maneuver).

Among the rules that should be given when trading cryptocurrencies that we have is not operating on illiquid pairs (which generate a trading volume lower than a minimum that is commonly established around 20BTC per day) and that of investing (only what you are willing to lose) always on projects that you know well and in which you have great confidence (so you have to study the various platforms, carry out your fundamental analysis and carefully choose which ones you want to operate on). In any case, before moving on, let's use a simple image to fix what we just said; in the following chart, therefore, we clearly see that the price moves within a "channel" delimited by two lines that respectively join the minimum peaks (the red line).

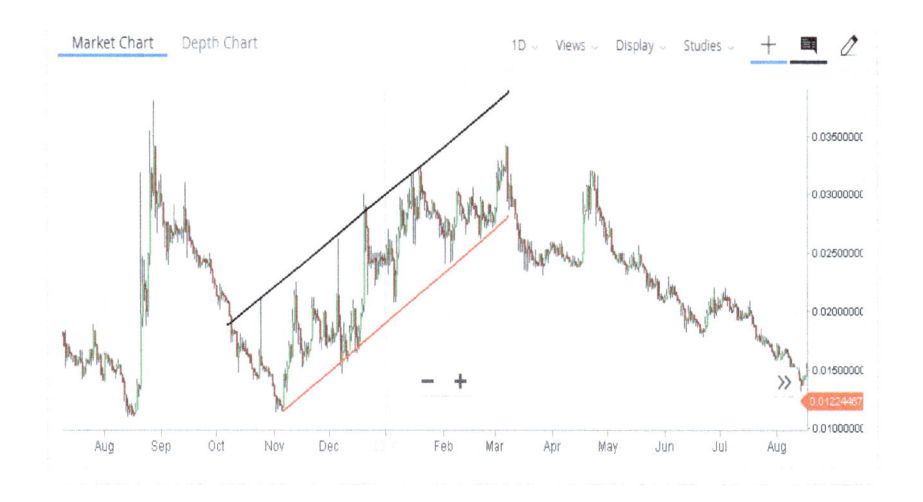

When at a certain point the price shows the first sign of weakness and does not show itself capable of going to test the resistance again (black line), here it tries to breathe for some time near the support; at this point, we are witnessing the last attempt at a bullish sortie, then the price suddenly drops, breaks the level (already tested several times previously), crosses the red line (the support) and enters a markedly bearish cycle in which at each new low one that is always lower than the previous one follows.

- **Relative Strength Index (RSI)**

We have said that every trader uses in his daily operations, a series of tools that help him to analyze the chart he is reading; these instruments can be divided into two broad categories, indicators (which freely replicate the price trend on the chart) and oscillators (which move in a defined range of values such as, for example, that between zero and one hundred). These tools (both indicators and oscillators) often provide us with very clear signals of what is happening to the price and their correct interpretation is what makes the difference between loss and profit.

The trading signals, however, we do not get them only from reading the data we get from the indicators and oscillators, but also directly through the price chart by plotting ourselves the levels that represent the "supports" and "resistances". Since for each currency pair on which we operate, we can change the unit of time (represented graphically by candles) we have a multiplicity of different signals depending on how we set the time frame (so technically, it is called the unit of time expressed graphically from the candle). For example, if we are trading on the BTC-ETH pair (i.e., we buy ETH by spending BTC).

Regardless of the modality, we use to obtain the trading signal, in the meantime, we must always start from the assumption that the signal is all the more solid the more the TF is set in an expanded manner; a chart with a one-week time frame offers more solid signals than a chart with a one-hour time frame.

If I wanted to buy ETH spending BTC, what I would do would be to wait for a moment when a trading signal appears on the 1W chart, start observing the lower TF, the one on a daily basis waiting to find favorable signals to buy also on this TF, then further reduce the time window to a 4-hour TF to find the exact point to open my position. To reduce the risk, we never rely on a single trading signal but we go in search of what is called "convergence" of the signals; if it is true, as they say, "many clues do not prove" it is also true that the more clues you have, the higher the chances of winning our bet. Because in a sense this is what we are doing, we are betting that the price going up; therefore, among all the tools used by traders, is there one that is simple to understand and that is commonly used and appreciated by the majority of the community? Yes, it's called RSI, an English acronym for relative strength index.

It is an oscillator that moves continuously between a minimum (equal to zero) and a maximum (equal to 100) invented by John Welles Wilder (who illustrated its operation to the public in 1979 with the book "New Concepts in Technical Trading System") and whose purpose is to help the trader identify the points where the strength of the trend is running out; the mathematical formula would help us understand why certain indications are obtained from the RSI, in any case, this does not change the operation, so, without complicating things too much, let's just say that the RSI moves between a minimum of zero and a maximum of one hundred, it reaches two ranges in which the trader's attention increases, the 0-30 range (which is defined as oversold) and the 70-100 range (which is defined as overbought).

When the RSI crosses the oversold and overbought ranges, it means that the market is in a phase of "excess" in which operators are essentially stubborn to sell and buy above reasonable (i.e., we are close to a price correction in the direction of contrary to that of the main trend). Unfortunately, to make a profit, it is not enough to rush to buy in the oversold ranges and sell in the overbought ranges, based on the strength of the current trend, in fact, the RSI can remain in "extreme" conditions (oversold or overbought) for periods of a very long time.

There are particular moments, however, in which anomalies are produced on the RSI if we compare the trend of the oscillator with what we read on the price chart. For example, when we see the price mark a low of $20, rise up to $23, and then return to mark a new low of $17, what we clearly read on the price chart is that by combining the two lows we obtain a descending line (which moves down); in certain circumstances, however, it happens that in conjunction with the two lows on the price chart, the RSI marks two peaks which, once joined, form an ascending line (which moves upwards).

This kind of anomaly is called "divergence" and is formed not only on the RSI but also on other types of oscillators and indicators (always in the same way); There are basically two types of divergences, the bullish ones (which can be read by drawing a line that joins the minimum peaks) and the bearish ones (which, on the contrary, can be read by tracing a network that joins the maximum peaks).

Any kind of divergence we notice between what we read on the price chart and what is expressed by the oscillator (valid for the RSI in this case but it is the same for almost all instruments) gives us a trading signal, in particular, if in a bull market we notice a divergence in the maximum peaks we have a sell signal (there is, therefore, the possibility of a trend inversion). If instead it is produced by combining the minimum peaks, we have a buy signal.

More technically we should then distinguish the divergences proper (two increasing peaks in the direction of the trend on the price chart in conjunction with two peaks in the opposite direction to that of the trend traced by the oscillator) from the hidden ones (in which the logic is reversed so the peaks expressed by the price are in the opposite direction to that of the trend, while the oscillator behaves in the opposite way); in the following graph, however, we will analyze only the classic divergences, while we will deal better with the hidden divergences in the paragraph dedicated to MACD. The RSI, in principle, offers us the best trading signals through the divergences that occur in the vicinity of the oversold and overbought ranges; such signals are more solid when they emerge on larger TFs (e.g. 1D and 1W).

A bullish divergence, for example, built on a chart with a one-week TF, in a strong oversold situation, and near solid support is almost always a good time to open a long position (basically buying our coins, then resell them at a higher price); the more signals we have that push us to buy, the more naturally we will be prepared to open a position. In any case, to simplify all this reasoning, below we graphically illustrate the functioning of two classic divergences (the first bullish and the second bearish); what we see in the green box is that the price on the chart marks three new consecutive lows while the RSI at those lows is rising (all this is graphically expressed by the red line).

As soon as the price (and the same thing happens at the same time as the RSI) breaks the resistance begins to rise and undergoes a rise of just over (at a guess) 30%; immediately after, however, in the black box, we notice that a bearish divergence is formed. On the chart, the price marks two new highs but the line that joins the respective peaks on the RSI (also in this case highlighted in red) is clearly descending.

This time, the support is broken and the price starts to go down. In the operation of a trader, the orange circles represent the moment in which it would have been advisable to open the position (the first two) and close it (the last two) to optimize profit and reduce any risks; this type of strategy does not always prove to be infallible so, by working exclusively with the divergences produced by the RSI, we will inevitably end up even getting into some bad situation.

- **Mobile Media**

What we must always have in mind when trading is that each chart offers us all kinds of signals (both bullish and bearish, both trend reversal and continuation) and it is up to us to interpret them correctly by making the different evaluations of the trend from time to time. When we collect a signal using the RSI, we should not be satisfied with this but we should go in search of confirmations using different tools to make sure that these also provide us with positive indications.

Among the most useful and at the same time simpler tools to integrate into everyday operations, we have moving averages; these tools do nothing but reduce the effect of random peaks by expressing the price trend on the chart in the form of a curve.

There are different types of moving averages, the most commonly used are called simple moving average (also called SMA or arithmetic) which assigns the same importance to all the values that the price assumes regardless of whether they are more or less recent, moving average weighted (WMA) which resolves the limit of the SMA by assigning greater relevance to more candles recent, exponential moving average (EMA) which assigns an exponentially increasing value to the most recent price values, and adaptive moving average which introduces the analysis of volumes in the calculation necessary to produce the curve that expresses the price trend. Regardless of the type of moving average, the curve that will be represented by the graph will have different appearance depending on the "period" that we have set; a 12-period moving average, for example, indicates that each point plotted by the curve represents the average of the last 12 candles.

Moving averages are therefore defined as "fast" and "slow" as the reference period increases; in this way, a 12-

period moving average (based on the prices of the last 12 candles) is considered a fast moving average and a 26-period moving average (based on the last 26 candles) is considered slow.

Moving averages are important precisely because we can create multiple moving averages with different periods by receiving different indications; in general, the periods most commonly used in technical analysis to track moving averages are 20-50-100 especially as regards the exponential moving average (which is the one that traders normally use the most). These tools offer us a quick and immediate glance at the market, when the price is above a moving average, the trend is for example considered bullish (on the contrary, if it is below, it is considered bearish); the trend is also considered as the more marked, the higher the period of the moving average above which the price stands.

This is because the moving averages also represent values of supports and resistances, the more solid, the greater the period used to build the moving average itself; another very useful indication that the moving averages give us is the way they intertwine with each other, which tells us a lot about the future course of the trend. Normally, when a faster moving average trims up a slower moving average, that is the time to buy; while on the contrary, the cut down is the time to sell.

Let's try to observe everything we have said on a chart (precisely a 1D chart of the BTC / XRP pair). Here, we have plotted three exponential moving averages at 20 periods (red curve), 50 periods (blue curve), and 100 periods (black curve) and highlighted (in green and black) two particular moments in the history of the price trend. Let's look at the first green rectangle, here at a certain point we clearly see the fast moving average (the 20-period one, colored red) cut up the two slower moving averages; the price immediately falls back using one of the slower moving averages as support and enters a markedly bullish cycle. In the second green box, we see the same dynamic with the price that first marks a big rise and then uses the slower moving average as support and returns to test the same resistance it had tested with the first rise; the development of the situation that we see unfolding in the green box is that either the price will break the short-term resistance (orange line) to then go and test the long-term one again (yellow line) or it will break the three supports represented by the three moving averages and it will fall back into the area of the last low (purple line) where in all likelihood it will either attempt a rebound or begin to build a divergence.

In the black squares, we observe the same dynamics but in reverse; in the first black box we can observe how the fast moving average cuts down the two slower moving averages one after the other with the price that once passed below it and it will begin to test the EMA100 (exponential moving average at 100 periods, the black curve in our chart) exactly as if it were a resistance.

In the second black box, the same scenario is repeated but with less vigor, the price seems, to gather around the moving averages but in the end, the bearish cycle prevails and the price touches its minimum peak; moving averages in general and exponential averages in particular, are extremely useful in traders' operations and if integrated into a broader strategy, they provide us with important indications on the possible future trend of the price.

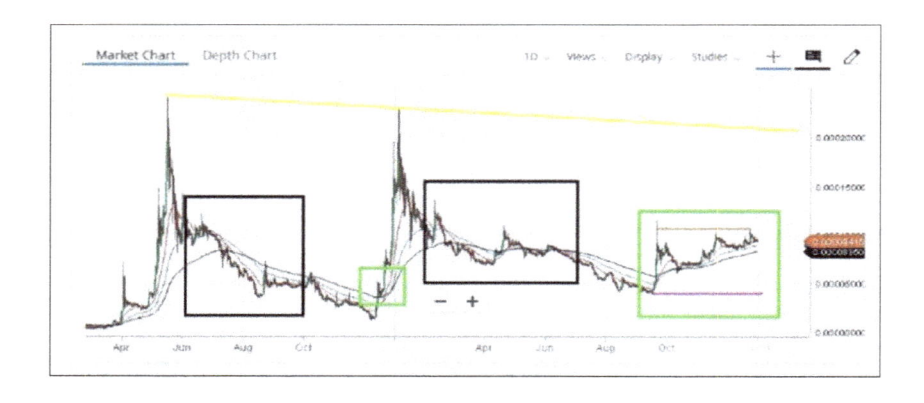

- **Moving Average Convergence / Divergence (MACD)**

In the previous paragraphs, we began to introduce the use of tools that should never be missing in a trader's toolbox; therefore, the MACD (acronym of "Moving Average Convergence / Divergence") could not be missing in this small overview.

We are talking about an indicator considered extremely useful by many traders who usually integrate it into their operations, built substantially on the basis of data extracted from three different exponential moving averages (at 9, 12, and 26 periods); one of the main uses of the MACD is to trace differences. Since in the paragraph dedicated to the RSI we have dealt with the classic divergences in this paragraph, we will deal specifically with that particular type of divergence that is defined as "hidden"; the dynamics with which the divergence is constructed are the same as we have seen previously, so also this time by joining the maximum (or minimum) peaks plotted on the price graph with a straight line, we will notice anomalies (the divergences in fact) compared to what we notice by tracing lines that join the peaks constructed by the MACD. The MACD is useful to us because it allows us to obtain more information on the strength of the trading signal, when we notice the same divergence both on the RSI and on the MACD, this is to be understood as an additional proof of the validity of the signal; the MACD then provides us with another interesting starting point, being graphically represented by the trend of two curves which are substantially two different exponential moving averages (EMA) normally highlighted with blue or black colors (for the slower moving average, at 26 periods) and with red color (for the fastest moving average)

Therefore, when the faster moving average cuts up the slower one we have a bullish signal, on the contrary, when the slower moving average is cut down by the faster one we have a bearish signal. In any case, as we have done in the other paragraphs, we use an image to fix the main concepts.

This time, we took two photographs of the market highlighting them with rectangles (green and black); in the first case (green rectangle) we see a typical hidden bullish divergence, in the second case (black rectangle) we always see a typical hidden divergence, but this time bearish.

As we can see the dynamics are identical to the one we described in the paragraph on the RSI, but this time in the green triangle we see that a new low is not marked and that the peak stops at a price slightly higher than the one reached in the previous minimum so that the line that joins the two peaks (colored blue) is ascending (therefore directed upwards); we find our beautiful hidden divergence by joining the minimums constructed by the MACD and obtaining a new line (also drawn in blue) which instead moves in the opposite direction (descending). The final outcome, regardless of whether the divergence is hidden or not, is the same, the price starts to rise and goes to retest the maximum peak reached previously.

In the black rectangle, we are witnessing a bearish scenario, this time the second peak fails to overcome the previous one, but stops a little earlier, so much so that the line (always blue) that we trace by joining the two peaks is descending (i.e. tends towards the bass); on the MACD we find our hidden divergence, joining the maximum peaks, in fact, our usual blue line this time is ascending (therefore, it moves in the opposite direction to the line that joins the peaks on the price chart since it points upwards).

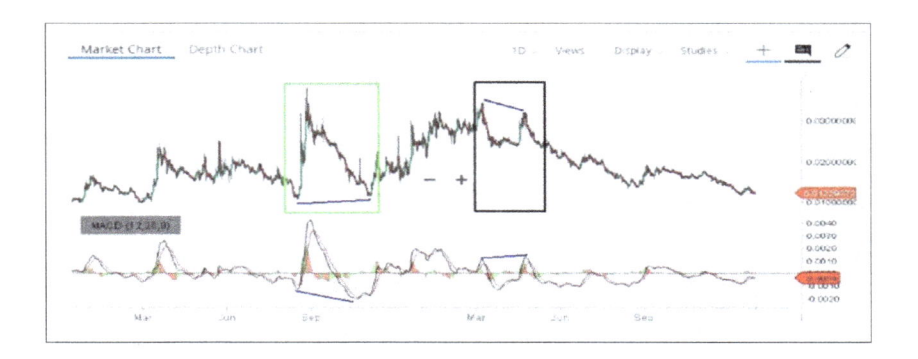

- **Ichimoku Cloud**

The tools we have described so far would be enough on their own to create a winning trading strategy;

associating the information we obtain with the supports and resistances to those obtained from moving averages, MACD and RSI we would already be able to trade in a profitable way, purely theoretically.

The final result, in fact, does not depend on how advanced the tools we equip ourselves with, but on how strict the rules we equip ourselves are; before describing a new tool, so useful how simple in the moment which you learn to use it, let's stop for a moment to summarize some of the rules we have seen and establish new ones. First of all, as we have already explained, you do not trade with amounts greater than what you are willing to lose; we also said that we should never operate on illiquid pairs (in which trading volume, as a guide, does not exceed 30BTC per day) and that we must always invest in projects that we know and in which we place great trust.

Some of the most important rules to follow concern the moment in which to close the operation, it can happen, for example, that during a trade the price breaks an important support and begins to plummet very quickly due to a sort of panic effect that overwhelms investors;

many traders, to cope with this circumstance, have a simple rule, which consists in never selling during dumps.

Selling when everyone is selling, in other words, rarely turns out to be a good idea and, more often than not, waiting for the price to rebound allows us to exit the trade with lower losses (or even a small profit); this brings us to a new rule which may seem trivial but which essentially consists in selling when it is time to sell. There are times when the price clearly demonstrates that it intends to go down even heavily, in those moments a smart trader agrees to close the position with a modest loss instead of being stubborn in a trade that in all likelihood will start putting him under great pressure soon.

When we open a new trade (and this is another good rule to follow), we should already have a fairly clear idea in our heads of the price we hope to sell at and the maximum amount of losses we are willing to tolerate if things should go bad; this simple rule of thumb allows us to put a stop to losses when things go wrong and to consolidate profits when things go well. Net of these small notions, however always very useful, we introduce a new tool which, although at first it may appear a bit chaotic, but actually allows us to interpret very easily and very quickly what is happening on the market; it is an indicator of momentum that takes the name of "Ichimoku cloud" literally "Ichimoku clouds", created by the Japanese journalist Goichi Hosoda. When a trader who has never heard of it finds himself observing the famous Ichimoku clouds for the first time, he usually feels a strong feeling of disorientation; as we can see from the image below, in fact, the graph is full of signs that must be interpreted in the right way.

However, it will be enough simply to describe what we see in the graph below to understand how simple the concrete use of this wonderful indicator is; the first thing we notice are those areas colored green and red, which are what are called "Kumo" (or clouds, in Italian). The perimeter of these clouds is delimited by lines (graphically represented with a darker color) which take the name of Senkou Span A and Senkou Span B. We can consider both Senkou Span (both A and B) as two averages mobile respectively to 17 periods (Senkou Span A) and 52 periods (Senkou Span B) both projected into the future of 26 periods. On the graph, then, we still distinguish two lines, this time outside the clouds, highlighted by the red and blue colors, which once again represent a pair of moving averages; the fastest moving average (9-period) is highlighted in blue and is called Tenkan-sen, while the slowest moving average (26-period) is highlighted in red and is called Kijun-sen.

We then note a last line of darker color, which faithfully replicates the price trend but which is positioned 26 periods behind, which is called Chikou-span (or delay line). This type of indicator provides us with many useful indications for trading and above all allows us to define at a glance whether the price is in an upward or downward trend depending on whether it stations below or above the clouds; other indications are then provided by the various crossings of the different moving averages and by the position of the delay line with respect to the clouds which represents a fairly reliable signal on the strength of the current trend.

As we have already seen, therefore, the best times to open a position are when the faster moving averages cut the slower moving averages upwards, while the position of the delay line with respect to the cloud is considered a signal of strength which can be either bullish (when the delay line peeks over the cloud) and bearish (when the delay line has now crossed the entire thickness of the cloud downwards and emerges from the opposite side).

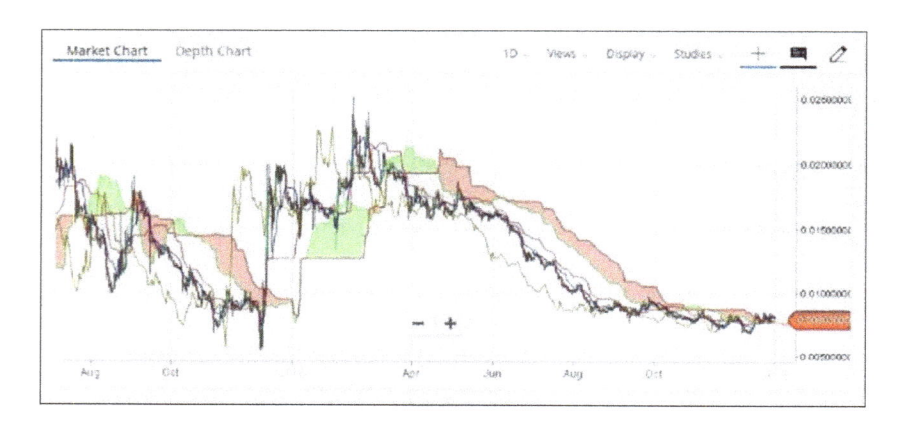

- **Parabolic Sar**

Selecting from all the tools that a trader has at his disposal, a small restricted group of tools to present to those who are completely fasting in trading is not an easy decision to make; my own "toolbox", so to speak, includes many other tools in addition to those I have had the opportunity to talk about such as the Fibonacci levels, the Pivot points, the Fractal Chaos bands and those of Bollinger, the Elder Ray Index, Klinger Volume Oscillator and On Balance Volume, Stochastic Oscillators and many more. Unfortunately, if we dedicated a paragraph to each of the tools that a trader can profitably use to develop his strategy, this would become a text on trading, which it is not.

Quite simply, this indicator, developed by Welles Wilder, allows us to understand when a trend is destined to stop; as we can see from the image, this instrument is graphically represented as a series of points that are positioned below the price line when the trend is bullish and above the price line when the trend is bearish. A trading strategy that correctly integrates the Parabolic SAR is to use other tools to define when we are close to a reversal of a bearish trend using the Parabolic SAR as a tool to define the moment of exit.

Normally, we will open our position when the Parabolic SAR is still above the price line and then later see it turn bullish; when the Parabolic SAR returns to position itself above the price line at that point we will have the sell signal we expected. In the following image, we can easily see how careful use of the Parabolic SAR allows us to maximize our profit; from the graph, we note that, in the rectangle highlighted in green, the price has placed two consecutive maximum peaks (in fact, the red line that joins them is ascending) while the RSI has formed two peaks in the opposite direction to the trend (in fact, the line red that unites them is descending).

Based only on the use of the RSI, therefore, noticing the formation of a classic bearish divergence, we would have placed our sale in a price range close to that highlighted by the blue rectangle. If, on the other hand, we had waited again for the Parabolic SAR to turn bearish, we would have sold about eight days later but at a price that this time would have been included within the range highlighted by the red rectangle.

Considering that between the lowest point of the blue rectangle and the highest point of the red rectangle there is a price variation that is around 30%, we understand well that using the Parabolic SAR in a rational way allows us to significantly increase our margin of profit. In this way, we begin to understand that we do not necessarily have to establish the sale price first, but we can also follow the trend as long as we always have a strategy that allows us to define the right time to close the transaction.

With this, we take the opportunity to throw them a couple of other valuable rules; in the first place, the rule that requires taking profit. If you never close the trade and continue to stay long waiting to land the blow that will allow you to increase your capital tenfold, you may have to wait a very long time, perhaps even forever.

Regardless of the trading style you use, even if you are a drawer and your operations can easily last for months, sooner or later the time comes when if you want to consolidate your profit you have to sell; if you never sell you never cash, it seems easy and yet it escapes many people. Another trivial but no less important rule to follow is that you cannot trade continuously; already doing any job without ever disconnecting is not exactly a healthy choice, doing something like this when it comes to trading simply means deciding to want to self-consume.

As we have often repeated, trading is an activity that subjects us to constant psychological pressure and if we want to make a profit, we must make sure that this pressure is tolerable or the stress will lead us to make a lot of mistakes; to understand how true this is, it will be enough to analyze the psychological response that every trader has when closing a trade.

Novice traders (who have not yet committed to mastering their emotional responses), when they close a trade at a profit get excited and feel as if they have discovered the secret to turning lead into gold. Loss operations make them become depressed and tend to lose confidence and self-esteem; this type of reaction induces the trader to continuously open new operations and what happens inevitably in a fairly long period of time, is that the trader eventually accumulates exorbitant losses.

What we must understand is that trading is not like gambling, all the choices we make must be carefully weighed before opening a trade, also, because after we open it, we can no longer do anything but hope that our analysis proves correct. An important rule to give us is to always take breaks between one trade and another, regardless of whether we have made a profit or not; in this way, we will have the time to metabolize all the accumulated pressure, study the errors eventually committed in our operation and look for a new one by weighing all the variables of the case with the utmost calm.

Personally, but this is very subjective, I impose a stop period of at least two days between the closing of an operation and the other, however, I myself do not always respect this rule; there are market phases in which there is an incentive to shorten or lengthen the stop period between the two operations, but the basic rule, in any case, is that you have to take breaks because it is not advisable, useful or even less healthy to trade every day from morning to night.

7. The Analysis Basic in the Cryptocurrencies Market

♦

In the last chapter, we have introduced some tools commonly considered essential to start trading; we also explained that there are still many other important tools to know how to use, which have not found space in this text but which should still be studied if you want to trade seriously.

In any case, we also had the opportunity to explain that a valid trading strategy that is capable of generating profit when practiced in a scientific manner does not necessarily have to be extremely complicated and sophisticated, but can also be extremely simple as long as it is based on rules. A trading strategy is therefore not simply reduced to the tools used for technical analysis but also includes all those rules (large and small, operational and not) that the trader imposes by himself with the aim of managing the pressures in the best possible way psychologically as this type of activity involves.